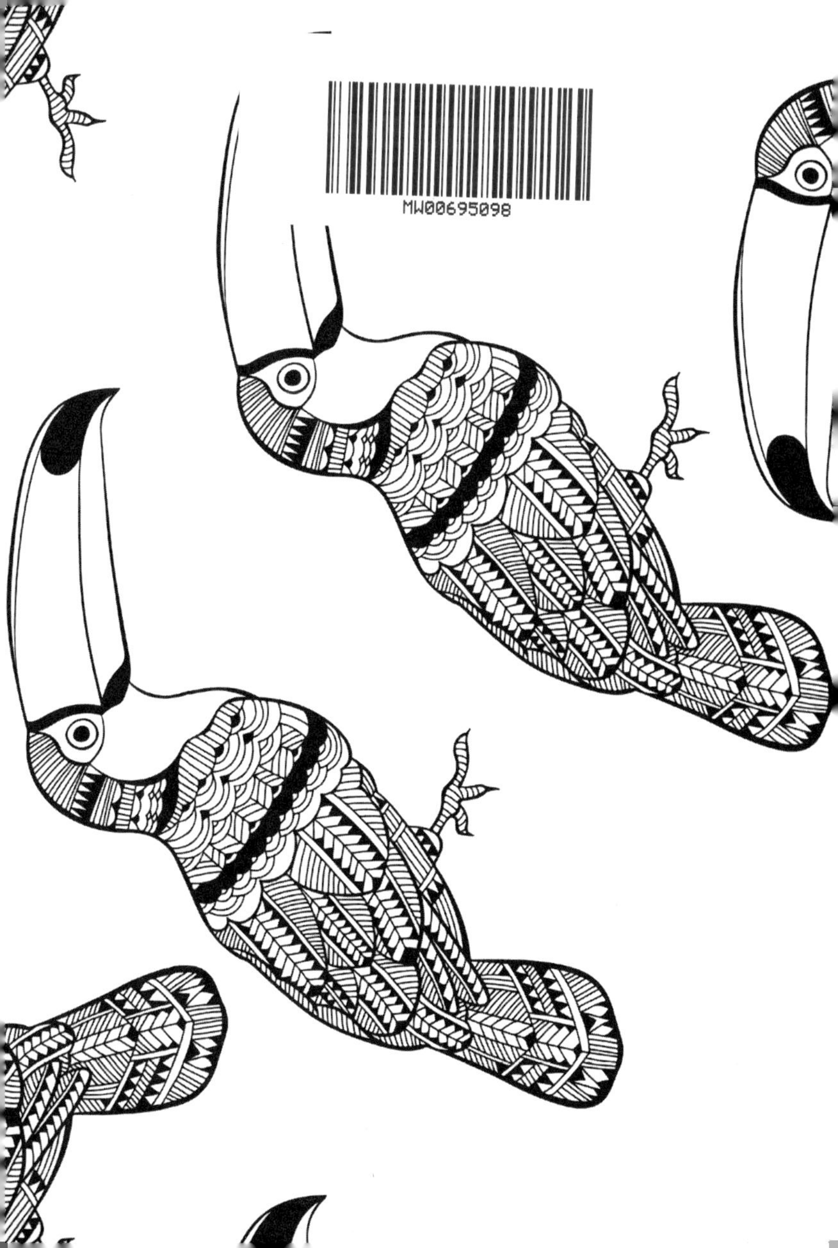

MW00695098

Tropical: 20 detachable postcards to color in
Hamlyn

Tropical: 20 detachable postcards to color in
Hamlyn

Tropicat: 20 detachable postcards to color in Hamlyn
© embra/iStockphoto.com

Tropical: 20 detachable postcards to color in
Hamlyn

Tropical: 20 detachable postcards to color in
Hamlyn

Tropical: 20 detachable postcards to color in

Hamlyn

Tropical: 20 detachable postcards to color in
Hamlyn

Tropical: 20 detachable postcards to color in
Hamlyn

Tropical: 20 detachable postcards to color in
Hamlyn

Tropical: 20 detachable postcards to color in

Hamlyn

Tropical: 20 detachable postcards to color in
Hamlyn

Tropical: 20 detachable postcards to color in
Hamlyn

Tropical: 20 detachable postcards to color in
Hamlyn

Tropical: 20 detachable postcards to color in Hamlyn

Hamlyn © milyana/iStockphoto.com

Tropical: 20 detachable postcards to color in © Vika17/Dreamstime.com

Hamlyn

Trapicat. 20 detachable postcards to color in Hamlyn © Irinakrivoruchko/Dreamstme.com

Tropical: 20 detachable postcards to color in

Hamlyn

Tropical: 20 detachable postcards to color in
Hamlyn

Tropical: 20 detachable postcards to color in
Hamlyn

Tropical: 20 detachable postcards to color in
Hamlyn